rocks
stones

FIND OUT ABOUT
Rock & Stone

© 1994 Watts Books

Watts Books
96 Leonard Street
London EC2A 4RH

Franklin Watts Australia
14 Mars Road
Lane Cove
NSW 2066

UK ISBN: 0 7496 1631 8

10 9 8 7 6 5 4 3 2 1

Dewey Decimal Classification 552

A CIP catalogue record for this book
is available from the British Library

Editor: Annabel Martin
Design: Thumb Design

Photographs: Eye Ubiquitous 23, © Bob Mazzer 4,
© Mike Southern 7, © P.Craven 8, © A.J.G.Bell 9,
© P.W.Hutley 13, © M.J.Frankland 18,
© David Cumming 20, © John Turner 29;
Chris Fairclough Colour Library 5, 12, 15, 17, 24;
Robert Harding Picture Library 16, 25, 28,
© Adam Woolfitt 14, © Bill O'Connor 30,
© John G. Ross 31; The Hutchison Library 26;
The Natural History Museum, London 26 (inset);
Science Photo Library / Julian Baum and
David Angus 6; ZEFA 10, 11, 19, 21, 22, 27.

Printed in Hong Kong

FIND OUT ABOUT
Rock & Stone

Henry Pluckrose

Watts Books

London • New York • Sydney

Whenever you wander
through woods,
run through grass,
paddle on a sandy beach
or walk along a city street,

there is something
in the ground
beneath your feet.
It is something we call rock.

Our earth is shaped
like a ball.
It has a hard outside shell.
This shell is made of rock.
Thick layers of rock
lie beneath the land
and beneath the seas, oceans
and rivers.

In places where there is
very little soil,
you can see some of the rock
which makes up
the earth's shell —
along the coast ...

in cliffs ...

and mountains.
These rocks were formed
millions and millions
of years ago.

We use rock in many ways.
Before it can be used,
it has to be taken from the earth.
Often explosives are used
to break the rock into pieces.

When the rock is
in small pieces,
it is cut into blocks.
These blocks of rock
are called stone.
The place where rock
is cut from the earth
and shaped into blocks
is called a quarry.

A person who works with stone
is called a mason.
A mason uses many different kinds
of tool to cut and shape the stone.

Stone is tough and hard-wearing.
It will not burn.
If stone gets very wet,
it does not go soft.

Thousands of years ago
people dragged these great stones
to Salisbury Plain.
They used them to build
this circle of stones
which we call Stonehenge.

Long ago, in Egypt, stone was used to build great pyramids.

Great castles and palaces
have been built in stone ...

and so have tiny cottages.

Stone has been used to build bridges ...

and, piled piece on piece,
to make a wall.
This wall was built
by the Romans.
It is called Hadrian's Wall.

Some kinds of stone
are good for carving.
Stone is used
to make statues ...

and for decorations
on the walls of buildings.

Marble is a stone
which can be carved and polished
until it shines like glass.

These slabs of stone are used
in quite a different way.
They have been laid
to make a pattern.

Some stone is so hard that it can be used to grind things into powder.

A knife-grinder uses a stone to sharpen the blades of knives, scissors and metal tools.

Some rocks contain gemstones,
like diamonds, sapphires,
emeralds, rubies and opals.
Deep tunnels, called mines,
have to be cut into the earth
to reach the rocks
in which the gemstones are found.

Gemstones are cut
and polished until they shine.
They are used in jewellery –
in rings, pendants
and brooches.

Have you ever looked carefully
at rock or stone?
You might see a fossil –
an animal or plant
that lived millions of years ago
before the rock was formed.

Have you noticed
that the small stones
you find on the beach
are often round and polished?
Their rough edges have been
worn away and smoothed.

Rock is part of the
natural world.
Some rocky outcrops
stretch upwards
towards the sky.
Climbers have to use
special equipment
to reach the top!

Rock was formed
millions of years ago.
But even the toughest rock
and stone
can be damaged
by polluted rain,
called acid rain.
We must take great care
not to destroy
the world in which we live.

About this book

This book is designed for use in the home, kindergarten and infant school.

Parents can share the book with young children. Its aim is to bring into focus some of the elements of life and living which are all too often taken for granted. To develop fully, all young children need to have their understanding of the world deepened and the language they use to express their ideas extended. This book, and others in the series, takes the everyday things of the child's world and explores them, harnessing curiosity and wonder in a purposeful way.

For those working with young children each book is designed to be used both as a picture book, which explores ideas and concepts, and as a starting point to talk and exploration. The pictures have been selected because they are of interest in themselves and also because they include elements which will promote enquiry. Talk can lead to displays of items and pictures collected by children and teacher. Pictures and collages can be made by the children themselves.

Everything in our environment is of interest to the growing child. The purpose of these books is to extend and develop that interest.

Henry Pluckrose